MICHAEL WILLIAMS

BOSSINEY BOOKS

ACKNOWLEDGEMENTS

I am very indebted to various people who have given me interviews for *Psychic Phenomena of the West:* the vast majority of these
accounts appear in published form for the first time. I am also
indebted to writers who have generously allowed me to quote from
their works. A special thank you to Mrs Mina Lethbridge for
unearthing the photograph of her husband Tom and letting me use
the last paragraph from his book *ESP Beyond Time & Distance*.
Thanks also to Ray Bishop and Eva Rutland for the cover, Felicity
Young for her drawings, especially commissioned for this publication, Lulu and Sally Dodd for their typing, and last but certainly
not least Pamela Guyatt for her thoughtful editing.

Photograph of Silbury Hill by Rob Scott
Cover photograph: 'Ghostly females greatly outnumber phantom
men ...'

First published in 1994 by Bossiney Books, St Teath, Bodmin, Cornwall

Typeset and printed by Penwell Ltd, Callington, Cornwall
© Michael Williams

ISBN 0 948158 92 1

ABOUT THE AUTHOR

– and the book

MICHAEL WILLIAMS, a Cornishman, started full-time publishing in 1975. He and his wife Sonia live in a cottage on the shoulder of a green valley just outside St Teath in North Cornwall.

In addition to publishing and writing, Michael Williams is a keen cricketer and collector of cricket books and autographs. He was the first captain of the Cornish Crusaders Cricket Club and is today President of the Crusaders. He is also a member of Cornwall and Gloucestershire County Cricket Clubs – and a Vice-President of the Cornwall Rugby Football Union. A member of the International League for the Protection of Horses and the RSPCA, he has worked hard for reform in laws relating to animal welfare.

In 1984 he was elected to The Ghost Club, and remains convinced Cornwall is the most haunted area in all Britain.

His recent publications include **Supernatural Investigation** *and, with Felicity Young as co-author,* **King Arthur in the West.** *In 1992 he also worked with Daphne Skinnard on a BBC Radio Cornwall series about Cornish legends and discussed the nature of ghosts on a Westcountry Television programme.*

In **Psychic Phenomena of the West** *Michael Williams examines a wide range of paranormal cases in Cornwall, Devon, Somerset, Avon, Dorset and Wiltshire. The supernatural and the sea, karmic astrology in Dorset, ghosts who will not go away, the work of Tom Lethbridge in Devon, and animals' psychic qualities are only some of the subjects featured. This, Bossiney's 221st title, shows how an important sea change is taking place in supernatural matters.*

IN October 1993 Sonia and I met Princess Narisa at her former family home, now Tredethy Country Hotel on the edge of Bodmin Moor. I had written about her late father Prince Chula of Thailand in Supernatural Search in Cornwall, *and the Princess told us on the night her mother died she was seen by people on the other side of the valley. Tredethy and the surrounding countryside have been the setting for varied paranormal activity.*

PSYCHIC PHENOMENA OF THE WEST

STRANGE powers are at work in the West. Dowsing and dreams, astrology and predictions, coincidences and claims of reincarnation, ghosts and phantoms are all alive and well – and these are only *some* of the subjects.

Healers are at work – men like Barney Camfield of Alphington near Exeter and Nelson Side of Camelford – and before the Doubting Thomases scoff and mutter 'mind over matter' it is well to remember that Nelson Side has done outstanding healing with horses. And for those wanting a look into the thing we call the future, there are prophets as different as Romany clairvoyant Acora and Italian-born Lori Reid, the professional hand analyst.

We are living through exciting moments in time when a whole range of findings are under the magnifying glass, revealing that the boundaries between what is real and unreal must be redrawn; and we must not forget time itself is the subject of debate.

For example there is no doubt that strange circles have appeared in Wiltshire cornfields and weird objects have travelled across the Wiltshire skies: there have been reliable human witnesses and photographic evidence. In my opinion, the more we investigate, the more sure it becomes that phenomena we call 'supernatural' genuinely do occur.

In the main, I have concentrated on cases and people in six western areas: Cornwall, Devon, Somerset, Avon, Dorset and Wiltshire, which happen to be our Bossiney publishing territory, but now and then I have gone beyond those regions for the sake of giving a more comprehensive picture.

The mind, of course, is the greatest mystery of all: the last frontier, the final unsolved piece in the puzzle of who and what we are. Our minds have powers which go beyond the five senses. Extra-sensory perception is a fact – but a fact still cloaked in mystery.

The idea that our human minds can transcend those five senses is no new concept. Unusual phenomena have always intrigued and fascinated.

Literature is rich in stories of psychic experience and in some instances – such as the case of Mary Shelley who dreamed the frightening experience of Frankenstein – it has been the inspiration of writing. We must also take into consideration the serious admission of Charles Dickens: many of his characters and plots came to him in his dreams.

Time and again in my investigations, though I have understood the reservations of the doubters, some of the facts relating to psychic phenomena are simply amazing.

What are they to make of time slips? There were the two English ladies who visited the Palace of Versailles in 1901. There they found themselves walking in the place as it was two centuries earlier: uniformed gardeners, costumed courtiers and all the buildings as they had been in the 18th century.

And what are they to make of psychometry? Here is just one case: a medium, David Young, was shown an early 19th century pistol. David Young knew nothing about the pistol, but after carefully handling it, he 'felt a connection' with the letters WE and the place name 'Brighton.' It transpired the gun had belonged to a man called West who had joined the army in Brighton.

And what about the coincidences?

Arthur Koestler wrote extensively about the search for a scientific explanation of coincidence. It was Koestler who coined the phrase 'puns of destiny' to describe the phenomenon.

Here is a modest case, drawn from recent personal experience. On Friday morning 25th of June 1993 I had been reading the proofs of a manuscript chapter, entitled 'Creatures of the Deep' for Ronnie Hoyle's book *Strange Tales of the South West*. Less than two hours later, in *The Times* and our local *Western Morning News*, I came across reports of recent sightings of the Loch Ness Monster – sightings by three people. Edna MacInnes and her boyfriend David Mackay saw the creature clearly, '...while driving near the loch this giraffe-like neck

rose from the water – it was only twenty feet from the shore...' Their story was backed by James Mackintosh, who, on a fishing trip on the same Tuesday evening, said 'I saw a brown giraffe-like neck sticking about six feet out of the water.'

Not only an odd coincidence, but another chapter in the long-running story: the first sighting on this twenty-four mile long loch by St Columba dates back to 565 AD.

The scientist predictably cannot accept strange tricks of fate. Take, for instance, the case of Charles Wells, an Englishman who became an overnight sensation in the 1890s. Mr Wells went to the famous Monte Carlo casino and not once but three times 'broke' the 100,000 franc 'bank' allocated to his particular roulette table. Incredibly, he was using no 'system.' Can coincidence explain why this unknown man was able to *sense* the winning numbers? We shall never know. After winning for the third and last time, Charles Wells disappeared into the night. He was never seen again, but lives on in that famous old music hall song *The Man that broke the Bank at Monte Carlo*.

◀ *THE WIDE skies of Wiltshire frequently have an aura of mystery – and with good reason. A number of reliable witnesses have seen strange objects flying over the landscape. Is science fiction becoming science fact? I have seen files and cuttings of UFOs, and it is difficult to dismiss all these accounts. The sheer volume of sightings in different countries around the globe means that more and more people are now looking at the whole UFO subject with open minds.*

THE SKIES of Dartmoor, like those of Wiltshire, have seen a fair amount of paranormal activity: claims of UFO sightings. This great wilderness is peopled by a number of ghosts, and the landscape has fired a good deal of creativity in words and paint. John Galsworthy who lived at Manaton, Sir Arthur Conan Doyle, Mrs. Bray (the wife of the vicar of Tavistock) and Beatrice Chase who lived an eccentric life at Widecombe, are only some of the writers who found inspiration on and around the moor.

GLASTONBURY TOR seen from Wearyall Hill. Some believe the female ghost seen in the vicinity of the tor is that of Queen Guinevere. If this is so, then it means Guinevere belongs to fact not fiction. It is a curious fact that although there are various Arthur place names in the Westcountry, there is no Guinevere location – yet she is a central character in the whole Arthurian tapestry. Within the context of the Grail Tradition, Arthur is about a search – our search – a quest to find our best self or selves.

Evidence and proof are often difficult words, especially in the field of psychic phenomena. Brian Inglis, the writer and television broadcaster, the man who invented the phrase 'fringe medicine' and championed the supernatural, wrote in the introduction to his magnificent book *The Paranormal, an Encyclopedia of Psychic Phenomena,* I have presented the evidence as if the events described actually happened. It would be easy, but tiresome, to hedge: with qualifications such as 'alleged' where, say, witnesses claim to have seen a person, or an object, floating in the air in defiance of gravity. I have preferred to work on the principle (which most historians accept) that if a phenomenon is reported sufficiently often by people of standing, its existence can be assumed, even if individual reports may be untrustworthy. Readers can make up their own minds from the evidence which reports can be trusted and which should be rejected.'

As an investigator I value first-hand witness above second-hand rationalisation. The fascination of the supernatural is that certain things occur and repeat – sometimes again and again – and yet they survive every attempt to exorcise or suppress them, or categorise them. And, of course, the supernatural is incredibly varied country, like the physical landscape we occupy. There are mountains and deep valleys, plains and rivers, but there is no such thing as a certainty.

I believe the strength of this publication is at an intensely personal level. Where and whenever possible I have allowed the people concerned to tell their experiences in their own words. This approach avoids generalisation and, in my opinion, strengthens the case for psychic phenomena.

Consequently many of these cases are appearing in published form for the first time, including my own odd encounter during the fifth month of 1993. Yet even that 1993 episode had a kind of ancestral experience some 28 years earlier. Sonia and I were then living at Bossiney and Linda Chesterman, a delightful neighbour of ours, described how she had seen this big black dog on the road high above Bossiney. 'The dog was so close to me that I could see it very clearly and yet it vanished in front of my eyes. There one moment, and gone the next.' Miss Chesterman later took me to the exact spot where she had seen this strange black animal. She assured me the dog had not leapt over any hedge. It had suddenly disappeared in the middle of a deserted country road. She told the story to a local farmer. He had no doubts: 'You've seen the ghost dog of Condolen!'

In the course of researching this book I met Melanie Corbett, the head custodian of Berry Pomeroy Castle. 'Despite the castle's haunted reputation,' she told me, 'I've never seen a ghost here but I am very aware of being watched by unseen eyes, especially when I open the property first thing in the morning, and workmen working here have felt the same.'

A parallel experience is that of Reginald Carthew who has worked at famous Jamaica Inn on Bodmin Moor for more than half a century. I have interviewed Reginald on two occasions and he confessed 'I've never seen a ghost here, but time and again I have been conscious of someone watching me... I'd look round and there'd be nobody there, but I was quite sure *somebody* had been watching me all the time.'

There is no doubt here in the West we have a high percentage of haunted locations. Lord Rees-Mogg, writing in *The Times* in August 1993, touched on this aspect. In a fascinating article entitled '*Homes*

STORIES of ghosts at Jamaica Inn on Bodmin Moor have rumbled on over the years. More than one person has felt an invisible presence here. I have wondered why numerous old inns claim ghostly residents. Could it be that many people have enjoyed many convivial hours in such properties and are therefore reluctant to leave them? Though some ghostly characters move about the majority are inclined to stick to a particular building or clearly defined area.

◄ *BERRY Pomeroy Castle.*

haunted by the Unknown Guest,' he reflected 'As I live in the Westcountry, I am thoroughly familiar with stories of ghosts; several concern houses which have belonged to members of my own family...

'John Wood, the elder, the great Bath architect, wrote that "the country around the hot springs of Bath have been particularly famous for its haunted houses"; that still seems true two-and-a-half centuries later. There seem to be one or two haunted houses in every Somerset village.'

Later I shall devote a chapter to ghosts who, seemingly, will not go away. In contrast there are manifestations who either fade gradually or abruptly from the scene and never come back. There is however a fourth category: those who are helped on their way.

Such a case came to me via a young Capricorn subject who lives on the edge of Dartmoor and is now serving in the RAF, stationed in East Anglia. 'We called him the Tuesday night ghost,' she told me. 'I and three other girls live in a 1930s style house just outside the station. My room is in the downstairs part of the house, and though none of us saw our Tuesday night visitor, all of us heard him. It was almost certainly a male ghost because the footsteps were heavy and loud; he might even have been an airman from the past. We became so concerned about these Tuesday night visits that we consulted the padre, and he explained that first of all we must really want to get rid of the spirit, as he called it. We were all agreed on that, because although we saw no sign of a figure, we all heard these footsteps ... it was very unnerving during the night, and oddly enough it was only on Tuesday nights ... you began to wonder if something in the past had happened on a Tuesday night.

'Anyway the padre came and prayed with another church person, and we've not had another visit on Tuesday or any other night. There was no ritual or any kind of service, just simply a prayer and that did it.'

My friend from Devon also told of a pub only a few miles away, 'where, as you go into the ladies toilets you feel an invisible person go past you ... she's thought to be a young girl.' This, of course, raises the interesting thought that there may be dozens of unseen ghosts hovering around us.

However deep and broad our learning, we can never begin to

15

understand everything in life – or death. But there is a strong something inside us – let's call it curiosity – which stirs us, encourages us to probe deeper.

The Bible says 'Seek and you shall find' – and a good deal of searching and finding is going on. It is all but 30 years since I had my first encounter with the unknown on the stroke of midnight at Bossiney. During the last three decades there has been an important sea change. Thinking men and women, critical assessors, are now looking at strange happenings with serious attention. The supernatural is no longer a hollow cause.

SOMERSET has a surprisingly large 'other population.' In my experience Somerset people are more ready to talk – or write – about paranormal activity than most. They have fewer inhibitions and generally look upon the supernatural as the supernormal. In certain lights there is almost another worldly quality about Somerset – as this photograph of Burnham demonstrates. Rosemary Clinch, the photographer, is the author of our Supernatural in Somerset.

A SUN DIAL made in 1792. Time itself is the subject of speculation. More than sixty years ago J.W. Dunne, author of the book An Experiment with Time, *worked along Einstein's idea that time is really the fourth dimension. He reasoned if time flows, then people must have a sense of some other form of time by which to measure it – this he called Time Two. In the supernatural realm there is no doubt whatsoever that time slips do occur: genuine experiences where people find themselves in the thing we call the past.*

GHOSTS WHO
WILL NOT GO AWAY

THE NATURE of ghosts is the problem. I have no doubt about the reality of ghosts – the evidence is overwhelming. More than a quarter of a century of investigation has convinced me of that.

But nobody, down the centuries, has conclusively answered the central question 'What is a ghost?'

In my last book, *Supernatural Investigation*, I devoted an entire chapter to the subject; putting that straight question to five people whose opinions I greatly respect in the supernatural field. They came up with some fascinating theories, but this truth remains: there is no single crystal-clear theory that can explain all manifestations.

We have to face the fact there are different types of ghosts: recurring manifestations – characters who keep coming back in ghostly form: historical ghosts who usually appear around old properties or ancient landscapes: modern ghosts, those of people or animals who have died fairly recently; even ghosts of the living; and, of course, there are haunted objects.

Because of the wide range of ghosts it is possible – even probable – that there is more than one explanation about the nature of these manifestations. Some believe we shall not get the full answer until we know what really happens after death.

Could it be that a ghost will, one day, give us the real answer?

In the meantime I am willing to settle for this: ghosts are manifestations of people or animals who have left this life – individuals who, in medical terms are dead.

They may appear real and quite solid or they may be transparent or insubstantial – or they may be in some scarcely recognisable form.

Though we shall always have the Doubting Thomases among us, I believe more people believe in ghosts today than at any point in man's history. We have come a long way since Dr Johnson on the subject of ghostly manifestation declared 'All argument is against it, but all belief is for it.'

But it's fair to say the Victorian age was probably the most haunted of all: those dark seances, the boom in astrology and fortune telling, the casting of spells. Ronald Pearsall in his thoughtful book *The Table Rappers*, published by Michael Joseph back in 1972, reflected 'The hauntings of Victorian England are extremely credible. They have the vestigial unfinished quality of dreams, and understatement.'

No less than Queen Victoria herself was attracted to the paranormal. My friend and fellow Bossiney author Peter Underwood has written a superb book *Queen Victoria's Other World*. This is the only book on the Queen's 'other world.' She was fascinated by death and certain she would be reunited with her Prince Consort on the other side. The strange and the unusual, every facet of the paranormal drew her like a magnet.

I have been investigating the supernatural since a few minutes before midnight on Midsummer Eve 1965; investigating, I trust, with a fair and open mind, with feet firmly planted on the ground of the here and now.

At this point, I want to concentrate on some places which somehow continue to trigger phenomena.

Berry Pomeroy Castle near Totnes is a good starting place because according to Elliott O'Donnell, the doyen of ghost hunters, he tracked down reports of hauntings here going back hundreds of years. This demonstrates incredible continuity of paranormal activity.

I first came to know about Berry Pomeroy Castle in the early 1970s when James Turner was researching his book *Ghosts in the South West* which David & Charles published in 1973. James never saw any ghost but he had the strong impression that the empty stone window frames of the ruin contained genuine glass windows as they had done all those calendars ago.

In 1982 I commissioned Peter Underwood to do his first Bossiney title *Ghosts of Devon*. Consequently I have visited Berry Pomeroy Castle at least once and usually twice on book business every summer since that year. Again and again in the last 11 years I have heard

I AM OFTEN asked 'Which is the most haunted area of Cornwall?' and never have any hesitation in replying, 'St Nectan's Glen.' Yet again we find ghosts near water, and reports of sightings date back to the reign of Queen Victoria.

of fresh sightings around the castle ruins.

For example, in July 1993 when I called at the castle cafe and shop, Olwyn Barker gave me these two accounts.

Glen Pomeroy from Stoke Gabriel, a descendent of the famous Pomeroy family, was signing the visitors' book on 19th June 1993 in the tea room, when someone tugged his sleeve but when he looked round there was nobody there. On a previous visit earlier in 1993 Mr Pomeroy took 24 photographs of the castle; 23 turned out perfect but the last had a shaft of light coming through it in St Margaret's Tower where there is no source of light – just the arrow slit!

On Thursday 8th July Rosalind Buttery, aged 13, came here. In her own words; 'I was passing the information room when I caught a glance of a shadow by the stair well. It was the left hand staircase. My father and I went down the staircase to investigate ... no one was there ... suddenly I began to feel hot and clammy.'

The point I am making is that paranormal presences have been reported here for centuries – quite simply ghosts that will not go away. It is, of course, possible that if people have believed something strongly for hundreds of years, then something of that belief may have left its mark. But even if we were to dismiss half the sightings as wishful thinking or some form of delusion, then the other half would represent a solid body of evidence.

Time may have something to do with psychic manifestation, but we should not expect ghosts to be governed by modern clocks and calendars. After all, the calendar was changed in 1582, and a year until then consisted of 355 days! For our part, the ghost hunters, it's often a matter of luck. We happen to be there when the ghost appears.

I have never had the luck to be in the right spot at the right time in St Nectan's Glen near Tintagel. This beautiful wooded glen high above Rocky Valley is the most haunted area in all Cornwall. My first interview about ghostly monks at St Nectan's was in the summer of 1965. Mary Bowley, a resident of Charmouth, Dorset, but a regular visitor to Bossiney, gave a very vivid account of seemingly alive monks walking along the path. In the autumn of that year Peggy Garside, a neighbour of ours at Bossiney, recalled her experience of monks suddenly vanishing into thin air, and a friend with her on that walk to the waterfall wrote to me confirming every detail.

Later I walked up the Glen with two well-known Westcountry spiritualists Alan Nance and Fay Glossop who 'tuned in' – the Hermitage, at the head of the glen, is reputed to be the site of a Saint's cell. We saw no phantoms, but Alan and Fay both found the atmosphere peaceful, spiritual, even energising, and they believed the monks returned because they loved the place so and felt benefit from returning. Though it is fair to say Alan had a very definite theory that people who returned to this world had not settled in the next – or had some unfinished business. Whatever the reason, the monks, to my knowledge, have kept coming back to the glen for more than 40 years, and Canon A.C. Canner, the former vicar of Tintagel, believed there had been reports of sightings dating back to the reign of Queen Victoria.

An interesting postscript to St Nectan's came in a conversation with Jean Litton in June 1993. Jean told me 'I was preparing food in the kitchen here and through an open door saw this dog walking back and forward, and though it looked very real, I knew it was a ghost dog because there was no paw sound ... absolutely silent. I wondered if this ghost dog was a kind of omen. Then three days later, within a matter of hours, Ben, our cross Alsatian Labrador, died suddenly. It was all very strange and there was something strange too about Ben in the glen; when he got to a certain point he always barked but there would be nobody there.'

The Bincombe railway tunnel, south of Dorchester, Sandford Orcas Manor House, Sherborne, the Bush Inn at Morwenstow near the Cornwall Devon border, and the Bedford Hotel, Tavistock, are just four other locations where ghosts simply refuse to go away.

DRIVING along a haunted Cornish lane. Several people have heard ghostly hoofbeats hereabouts – and there has been a definite sighting of the ghost horse by two people. Whether walking or driving, I've found this a perfectly normal lane. Rebecca Pickford and I did an interview at this location for part of a BBC Radio Cornwall series, and Rebecca agreed: 'No haunted feeling here.'

MARILYN PRESTON EVANS

HEALER AND UFO OBSERVER

MARILYN PRESTON EVANS, who lives at Saltash just above the River Tamar, is not only a great animal lover but healer of animals. Her long list of patients include dogs, cats, birds and human beings. Her other special interest is UFOs.

Recently she allowed me to read her manuscript *Another World* and generously suggested I might like to use some extracts in this book. The following entries underline the diversity of her life.

'On Saturday 27th December, 1980, a UFO passed over our house early in the morning, whilst our two dogs had been very restless and whining, which fortunately was most unusual. I took the dogs out to the front garden, and there, in the early morning sky, a scintillating ball of coloured lights was slowly crossing the sky from west to east, the outer ring twisting one way as the inner part was revolving the opposite way. Watching it as it silently disappeared, I wondered what its mission was and where it came from. The dogs quietened and we all came in again.

'At 9 am I telephoned a full description of what I had seen to the news room of the *Western Evening Herald* in Plymouth and the following was published on Monday, 29th December, 1980:

'Woman spots UFO over Saltash.

'Another UFO, spotted over Saltash on Saturday, may be connected with a series of Christmas Day sightings throughout the Westcountry. Mrs. Marilyn Preston, of Higher Port View, Saltash, shortly before dawn on Saturday saw a bright light in the sky. Much bigger than a star, it was "twisting within itself" and changing colour as it crossed slowly from west to east, said Mrs Preston. 'Like the lights seen in Devon and Cornwall on Christmas Day, it left a

MARILYN Preston Evans, centre, enjoying a joke with friends at a crop circle gathering in Bickington, Devon 1990.

"vapour trail" but this one took several minutes to cross the sky. RAF Mount Batten have dismissed the earlier sightings as a meteor or a satellite breaking up, according to Plymouth UFO Research Group chairman Mr Bob Boyd, but he disagrees.

'"Four people have called me about the lights they saw, and in one case a man said he saw them coming from west to east, then turn in a big curve", said Mr Boyd. "A satellite would not do that."'

Marilyn strenuously maintains that she has had contact, through astral projection, with a man, dressed in a one piece space suit, who has landed here from a space ship. More than once I have asked her whether these were dream experiences but she insists that though her physical body was home in bed this was reality experience.

In her manuscript she refers to a radio interview on the subject of animal survival after death which I did with her and Ken Snowdon.

Somehow the conversation got around to her UFO experiences and I asked for the name of her UFO friend. She confessed she did not know his name. Here is how she continues this part of her manuscript.

'Next morning our telephone rang – it was Doris, our lovely medium friend from Plymouth. "Marilyn! I must tell you! Your beautiful space friend has come to me in my meditation this morning, in a great golden light – he asked me to pass on a message to you – that his name is Janus." She continued with some excitement, not knowing that I had been interviewed the day before for a radio programme and had been asked that very question. "I queried the name and he wrote it, in gold, for me to see and pass on to you, saying you needed to know."

'You may perhaps, imagine my delight at this news – and also in the fact that he was obviously aware of the previous day's interview, and went to Doris, as I was obviously too thick to receive his mental message personally!

'It does give further credence to the truth of such happenings. If the name had popped into my head, it could well have been accepted by others as "imaginings" but for that to have happened to Doris, who was quite oblivious of the interview and that particular question, and to be asked by Janus to pass on this information because it was needed by me, shows there is so much more to all these things than meets the eye. One more little piece to the huge jigsaw!'

Though conventional medicine – for animals and humans – is now much more tolerant of spiritual healing – or whatever we call it – people still ask me 'Does it really work?'

Here are just a few brief cases from Marilyn Preston Evans' manuscript.

'In the month of March, 1971, my father-in-law's 14 year old dog, Robbie, was taken ill with a stroke. The power in his back legs was gone. After examination, the vet, said the dog was too far gone and the best thing for it was to be put down. We heard of Mrs Preston and we took the dog to her. After four visits and the dog being on her absent healing list, the dog is now running around, and also getting up and down steps ... we are very grateful. NGE, Devon.'

'This is to recount my own personal experience of spiritual healing with Mrs Marilyn Preston of Saltash. Earlier this year, I took one of the children's pet cockerels to her, suffering from a deformed foot. The bird had been walking on a stump as the toes of the foot had turned inwards, and indeed the toes seemed to be withering away. The cockerel had been like this some two months or more, and the verdict of knowledgeable poultry keepers around, was that it should be 'put down' as it could only hobble and was being tormented by the other birds in the flock. Mrs Preston kept it some ten days at her home. When I called to collect the bird, the foot was no longer turned under but was, to all intents and purposes, a normal cockerel's foot with claws stretching to the front. The bird itself was in good spirits. Since then, although we expected the foot to revert to its previous position, this has not occurred and the bird today walks normally and perches, and is, in fact, very well able to take care of himself! Looking at him now I do not think anyone would know that he had once suffered a deformity. He has needed no further treatment since Mrs Preston had him. I am open minded as to the significance of spiritual healing, but I am certain in this particular instance Mrs Preston was able to effect a miraculous cure. I would not hesitate to take any sick animal to her in the future. PA (BBC)'

These next three examples concern people.

'Following a fall while playing cricket during August,1970, I damaged my shoulder and upper arm. After a few weeks of considerable discomfort, I visited my family doctor who examined me, and considered that I had a severely pulled muscle. He then prescribed a course of tablets, but all this was to no avail. I had difficulty in sleeping, the pain was considerable and I could not even pick up a telephone directory. I again visited him during February and he arranged for me to have an X-ray. Apparently no bones were broken, and he then arranged for me to have therapy treatment at hospital three times a week for a month. Although this treatment strengthened my arm somewhat, I still experienced the pain and discomfort, and with the cricket season again with us at the end of April, I could not throw a cricket ball at all, and even with trying, it was like someone cutting my arm off.

'However, a friend of mine who was taking his wife to see Mrs Preston at Saltash, suggested that I made an appointment to see her. I'm afraid I had no confidence whatsoever in spiritual healing, and actually considered this more of a joke. I was, however, at the stage when I was prepared to try anything, and he made the necessary appointment with her. After my first visit the pain moved rather suddenly from my upper arm to my shoulder. This I mentioned when I visited her again the following week, and from that visit, although I did go once more, I have been completely free of pain, and I can now sleep without any trouble, throw a cricket ball as well as ever I could, and now, after some four months, I feel really fit and well.

'I have no alternative than to give Mrs Preston full credit for my recovery, when all orthodox treatment tried had been unsuccessful and I now have every confidence in the healing she is giving to humans and animals alike. MH'

'I have suffered for the last five years with rheumatoid arthritis, according to the doctors. I have had three operations which I admit have helped. But I was still getting pain in the top of the spine and neck. Also terrific migraine. I then went to see Mrs Preston of Saltash. She gave me spiritual healing. Almost at once I began to feel better. This was in May, 1971. I went to see Mrs Preston approximately four times. I am thankful to say I am now completely cured. I haven't seen a doctor since. Also I am now doing a full time job as a waitress. I did not believe in spiritual healing before; I still don't understand it, it seems rather uncanny to me, but the results must prove that Mrs Preston has some healing powers that the ordinary person has not. SC'

'Two years ago I had patches of rash appear on my legs. I received treatment from my doctor. The condition worsened and spread to my arms and body. In November, 1970 the condition became acute. I was still being treated by the doctor; it then affected my scalp and hands. I became extremely depressed, still having treatment. In May, 1971, I got in touch with Mr DM in Plymouth, who advised me to see Mrs Preston. By then I had lost faith in man and God. Now I am well again. No depression, my faith restored, the rash cleared, excepting for a small area of dry skin on both heels. I saw a skin specialist on September 14th who confirmed that I had psoriasis which is considered incurable. He was extremely impressed by my mental and physical condition. I was very sceptical of the spiritual faith – now I am a firm believer. I have had no orthodox treatment since May 1971. LB'

THE BLUE Anchor Inn at Cannington, Somerset, is one of many Westcountry hostelries with a haunted reputation. If, as many students of the supernatural believe, nothing is ever truly lost – everything we say, do or think is preserved – then it is reasonable to suppose things from the past might return to their old haunts. There is no doubt people in inns, pubs and hotels do pick up sights and sounds from earlier days. There are also odd happenings like lights coming on or taps running – relatively minor events in themselves but all somehow defying logical explanation.

STRANGE ENCOUNTERS IN WEST CORNWALL

RUPERT WINSTON SPARROW is a writer, painter and illustrator who lives in Carbis Bay, West Cornwall. Over the years he has gathered together a rich harvest of true supernatural stories relating to the region, and he has kindly allowed me to quote three examples. The first two concern Mary Williams, the well-known St Ives author who also paints and illustrates.

'Some years ago when I was walking back from Zennor to St Ives, I had an experience which even now cannot be explained rationally. Normally I took the field path, but that evening, as a mist was rising, I started by road, at a point I knew well. I climbed the low stone wall to a patch of rough moorland, which meant cutting off a corner and joining the winding road further on. For a few minutes everything was normal. Then, as I continued, with the mist wreathing against my face, waves of cold fear slowly enveloped me. I have used this path many times without anything untoward happening.

'This time, as one does when one cannot see in front of one, I put my hand ahead, and to my shock came against the old branches of a tree! I stepped aside and ran into a bush. Again I tried, but whichever way I chose, I was surrounded by the twisted grasping arms of low trees which in my upset state assumed the identities of malevolent creatures imprisoning me in a cage of elemental evil. If I had not known the walk so well I would have told myself I was merely off route; but I knew I wasn't, just as I knew that there were no trees near that particular spot of ground! How I eventually reached the road again, and how long it took, I have no idea. But when I did, I was shaking with terror and had to wait for some moments before walking on, almost running, towards St Ives.

*IN MY experience areas strong in atmosphere seem to trigger psychic phenome-
na, and the Zennor district is such a case. There have been happenings hereabouts
that defy all logical explanation. Zennor, in certain conditions, generates the feeling that you are at the very edge of the unknown. Interestingly too, the place has
inspired a good deal of creativity: painting and writing. The moors running
down to the edge of the Atlantic add to the drama, and it is worth reflecting that
D.H. Lawrence lived here for a while during the 1914-18 war and was then
hounded out because of his German wife, his anti-government views and allega-
tions of lights signalling out to sea at night.*

'The next day I returned to Zennor, and as the mist had cleared and
it was a beautiful afternoon, I determined to retrace my steps of the
previous evening. The hills were burnished gold and copper in the
autumn sunlight.

'I climbed over the wall in the exact spot as previously, taking the identical path. There were no trees there ... no bush in sight, nothing but bracken and tumbled stones in the undergrowth. Under the clear sky the landscape looked friendly and welcoming, as though, with the lifting of the mist, its sinister evil had gone to earth and slept.

'Do one's thoughts become concrete things? Can we imagine to the point of creating our own terrors?'

Rupert Winston Sparrow and I both share a deep interest in animal welfare. This is why we are fascinated by Mary Williams's second account: a strange animal encounter in the same area of West Penwith.

'There is a ruined chapel ensconced by bracken and gorse along the field path from St Ives to Zennor. There I had a further sinister experience on a walk back from the latter. It was again, late afternoon, and as I neared the ruin I looked up and something with pointed ears silhouetted against the sky peered watchfully from the top of one wall. I wasn't frightened, though a little apprehensive. The contour was fox-like, dark. But a fox would hardly have climbed that erection of rocks ... besides, the ears were slightly curved at the sharp tips. I went on quickly. When I looked back the head had disappeared. There was no sound, no rustle of footsteps; only the dying sunlight throwing its last gold over the wold landscape.'

I have long had a hunch that places, strong in atmosphere, are most likely to trigger manifestations. Carn Kenidjack is such a location: a mass of piled shattered granite capping beautiful moorland abut a mile and a half north east of St-Just-in-Penwith.

Kathleen Bradshaw came here one day with her husband. She left him at the top and went down the slope to pick some flowers. Returning, she was surprised to see a number of people in white mackintoshes surrounding him. As she climbed the slope to rejoin him, the people in white had gone.

'Who were the party of people?' she asked.

He looked at her strangely. 'Party? No one has been here. I've been alone all the time.'

But Kathleen Bradshaw had no doubts: 'I saw them very clearly ... no doubt at all ... yet he never saw *anything*.'

A time slip? A Druidic circle perhaps?

LOOKING down on St Just-in-Penwith and the Atlantic from Carn Kenidjack. Here is another example of power in the landscape. Generally there is a brooding quiet about the place. I have been here at different times and different seasons, and felt its atmosphere to be strongest in that mysterious hour between sunset and the closing in of darkness.

JUDY HALL with an old friend in the Sekhmet Temple in Egypt, which has featured prominently in her past life memories.

JUDY HALL

JUDY HALL has been an astrologer for twenty years. She pioneered karmic astrology in Britain, and today runs a flourishing karmic counselling practice from her home in Thomas Hardy's Dorset. She also writes and runs workshops to explore past lives.

I began by asking her about the nature of her work: 'I believe that we are here to balance out our karma, to clear up the deficits, yet but above all to grow and move forward and you can't do that if you are bound on an inexorable wheel,' she told me as we sat overlooking a magical stretch of water on a light grey September morning.

'Once you realise that everything you do contributes to, and creates, the future, you start to be a lot more careful. I feel that we can, indeed must, move beyond karma and that this is what the *New Age of Aquarius* is all about. My work is very much focused on helping people to release their karmic past and fulfill their purpose in incarnating.

'I've always been interested in visual imagery and have used it as a tool for self-healing and for exploring the past, as well as for attuning to the energies of the Zodiac.

'I was psychic as a child; I was always seeing things: flashbacks and "ghosts". Both my grandmothers were psychic but my mother was frightened by it so I didn't understand what was happening and picked up her fear. However she's mellowed.' A broad smile. 'I'm a Sagittarian, typical of my sign, never stop asking questions. I'm on a quest, always finding answers or trying to find them. My astrological chart is a bowl ... so I suppose it's all tied up with a kind of Holy Grail ... always looking for the spiritual essence.'

You sense there is something of the detective in her – those brown eyes seem to miss very little. You soon discover she is a superb inter-viewee – words flow naturally. On the evening of our interview, she was appearing on television.

She is the author of *The Karmic Journey: The Birthchart Karma and Reincarnation*, co-author with her partner of *The Wise Woman: a Natural Approach to Menopause*, and most recently *The Zodiac Pack, A Visual Approach to Astrology*, and *The Astrology of a Prophet? The Horoscope and David Icke*.

She studied psychological astrology with Howard Sasportas and lectured with him on the karmic aspects of astrology. She has also been working with an author who has researched the first World War poet Wilfred Owen. They have linked his life, and his poetry, to his birthchart, throwing new light on his death and purpose in living.

A major influence in her life was the mystic writer Christine Hartley.

'Her book *A Case for Reincarnation* opened the door for me. I just devoured the book, and arranged to meet her. We met in a restau-rant, and after a while Christine said "This may be the first time we've met in this life, but we've sat together like this so often over the centuries".

'The young waitress almost dropped a plate of food all over me. Twenty years ago, you couldn't discuss these things so openly and loudly as you can today. Christine Hartley took me on as her pupil and taught me the whole theory of reincarnation and regression ther-apy. She worked in magic, very different to her outward life as an uppercrust old lady.

'Her father had been one of Queen Victoria's doctors, although he was totally against anything "psychic". It's interesting to think that the old queen all those years ago was so preoccupied with "the other side". I have a feeling that they were quite happy to go along with the paranormal, but didn't consider it something suitable for the lower orders!'

How does she describe herself?

'A karmic counsellor ... it's looking at past patterns shown in birth charts and past lives. I also take people back to earlier times.'

Does she hypnotise them to do so?

'No. You achieve this going back by a meditative technique. You're trying to get in contact with the higher self, the part of yourself that

WELLS, a place which Judy Hall recognised from an earlier life, but where she noted certain changes. That is perhaps inevitable. Yet Wells remains a jewel in the Westcountry crown.

knows and it's vital that the person *needs* to know. I believe hypnosis bypasses that need. With my technique the control remains with the person undergoing the experience.

'A karmic reading, which I do on tape, is an in-depth study, shedding new light not only on your soul's purpose in incarnating but also on relationships, emotional or health problems, and the stumbling blocks in life. It's a combination of astrology and psychic reading. It pinpoints relevant lives and patterns of behaviour carried forward from the past.'

Why do people come to her, or make contact with her?

'There are three main categories. The first and biggest group is "Why am I in this relationship? Or why am I *not* in this relationship?" The second group asks "Why this illness?" And then the third category "What's holding me back?" Or, more rarely, "What is my purpose?" The biggest percentage is in that first group: relationships or lack of relationships.

'Each incarnation can be seen as a learning experience set up prior to birth in order that the strengths and wisdom acquired in previous lives can be used to overcome inherent weakness and areas of imbalance.'

Is there such a thing as a success rate or is that just an impossible question?

'I've been doing this work for twenty years and in that time I've done hundreds. Only three people have said "Rubbish!" although some people find it difficult to accept past lives, I don't believe all remembered past lives are true anyway. In this field it's very difficult to quantify terms like success and a lot of people don't give you any but may say "Things have become different ... better in some way." And that's gratifying because so many of them needed to change direction. Certainly many phobias and karmic illnesses have been cleared as well as healing relationships and family patterns.'

She and her partner, Robert Jaslus, live in Wimborne St Giles, a village which is in itself a trip back into the past. Judy has a strong sense of connection to a previous era and lives in the house she had always dreamed about; and she knows she has had several past lives with her partner.

Robert, a doctor trained in conventional medicine, now practices complementary medicine. Despite his uprooting from the orthodox path, the local health authorities pass on patients for his attention, and he and Judy often work together on the roots of a patient's disease.

She agrees that Dorset has a strong supernatural quality. 'The earth energies are particularly strong and the past is very close to the surface. We have a ghost car near us. It's broken down and people drive into the back of it, damaging their own car in the process. They dash off to phone a garage and come back to find the car gone and there's nothing wrong with their own. People keep mentioning this to me "in confidence" because they don't think anyone else will believe it!'

A Bronze Age horseman has appeared hereabouts, on the Dorset Cursus and Roman soldiers have been seen further down the old Roman road, Ackling Dyke. One of her favourite Dorset locations is Knowlton Circles, an ancient henge with its ruined Norman Church, five and a half miles north of Wimborne.

'There is this tremendous atmosphere – so energising. A local magazine article recently said it was haunted, but "full of presences" would be a better description. It evokes the ancient past so strongly. My four year old grand-daughter loves coming to the circle.

'When she was about two and a half she told me we had once lived in a small room above the church porch, now just a small stone wall that she loves to sit on (it incorporates one of the old stones).

'I've had many "pictures" of Knowlton, once a major ritual site with four henges, without the church and with a stone circle within the ditch. The Society of Dowsers recently marked the position of the stones, exactly where I'd seen them.

'My house lies on one of the energy points, as does my daughter's. Growing up on a leyline, it will be interesting to see what emerges in my grand-daughter's life.'

Across the border, she enjoys an attunement with Somerset. 'I was present on Glastonbury Tor when they hanged the last abbot there and I consider both the abbey and the Tor a spiritual home.

'I've had some glimpses of much earlier lives, including a ritual submersion in the Chalice Well. On researching this later, I found out there is a kind of ledge and a space just big enough to take a person standing upright. That still gives me the shivers and I haven't really wanted to explore it further. I'm also totally convinced that

I've taken part in rituals inside the tor, as well as being a hermit on its slopes, and a very ordinary monk at the abbey.

'I met the Chancellor of Wells Cathedral some years ago and we did a tour of the building and the Bishop's Palace, a very powerful place for me. I was able to point out how certain things had changed. "You've not been here since the 15th century!" he said. I found a seat in the chapter house which I had used as a prebendary – mainly an administrator – in a previous life.'

Judy has crystal-clear pictures of earlier lives. 'It all started when I had a near death experience in childbirth. Alarm bells were sounding, nurses and doctors scurrying around ... and I was able to watch it all from the ceiling. I relived a time when I was a woman who had had a lot of children in abject poverty and died in childbirth. This time I decided to get on with it as I didn't want to have to come back and do it yet again!

'Then there was an experience in medieval France when, as a young girl, I was being hunted by a man in armour on horseback ... a very frightening experience ... but there was a partial eclipse and I was able to escape. I later drew the designs of the armour, and the College of Heralds confirmed it was 13th century, and the Royal Observatory confirmed there had been a partial eclipse on the precise date. I had many more glimpses of the same life. Later I read Arthur Guirdham's book on the Cathars and it all fitted. And when I went to Egypt for the first time, it was like going home ... echoes everywhere of things that had gone on before.'

What about ghosts?

A thoughtful silence: 'There seem to be ghosts and ghosts. In many instances it's like an imprint held, as an old film holds an image. Just the memory left. At other times the spirit is still trapped there. In my time I've done a lot of rescue work ... talking to them, helping them to move on. Other spirits are very active. They are here to help.'

Some people are colour blind. I get the impression others are blind in another sense. We may call it supernatural or spiritual. What does she think?

'I agree entirely. Some people are blind in these matters. They don't either recognise or understand ... and this is very true of reincarnation and past lives. Some are very sceptical. Others can handle it only at arm's length. I have to admit when younger they had to drag me into a spiritualist church! But when I got there it was like coming home and I learned to value my psychic abilities and, what is more important, to use them for the benefit of others. I feel that these are natural abilities but, because of the church's opposition, they have been suppressed. Now they are beginning to emerge again. For me, they are a part of our spiritual heritage from a distant past and we need them in order to attune to the spiritual part of ourself.

Has she met many people claiming to be famous characters in the past?

'Not all that many. Though I have met people who said they were Lord Palmerston, Boadicea, Gandhi and Tutankhamen amongst others. Curiously enough, Judas keeps cropping up. I don't for one moment believe all these people were Judas but there seems to be a clearing out of betrayal going on – appropriate for the end of the Piscean age – and the more I uncover the more I'm inclined to think Judas was a scapegoat that people who carry this pattern tune into. That's probably a dangerous thing to say to conventional church people. When I did a Religious Studies degree back in my college days I think my tutor thought I should have been burnt at the stake! Indeed, I'm sure in a past life he had been an inquisitor who sent many heretics to the flames!

'Seriously though, it is very sad that religion is the cause of so much war and bloodshed in the world. Take, for example, the problems in Ireland. If we could get some of the opposing sides back to earlier lives, and different religious affiliations, then I believe the whole thing could be cleared up.

'Many people suffer the same problem over and over again. With the help of karmic astrology, they can recognise the reasons why, find a new way to deal with it, and then move on. Karmic counselling can help us all to realise that we are spiritual beings on a human journey. It puts us in touch with our soul's purpose ... and points the way to new growth and integration.'

How does she operate?

'Various ways. People can come and see me in Dorset for a regression by appointment. Or I can send them a reading on cassette through the post. And then I do workshops; these are usually two

41

days although I do week long ones in Greece. We start off by getting people comfortable – that's important as they have to trust each other and me – and then it's a matter of tuning in to an inner guide, a general clearing process and focussing in on the past life information and the healing process.

'I hold workshops all over the place in the north, in Cornwall, and overseas countries like Germany and Greece. I prefer to work in small groups, but the range of personality and occupation is enormous: consultants of all sorts including psychiatrists, actors and accountants and therapists, people who call themselves "ordinary housewives", and all ages from 18 to 83.'

And what does she hope to achieve?

'In a modern sentence: "Throw a bit of light on it." A knowledge of previous lives and the plan for the present lifetime is a very potent tool. Helping people to change their pattern is important. Sometimes they come through sheer curiosity, but usually there is a problem and another person or other persons are involved. Basically they want to go back and find out *why?*'

CHESIL BEACH is more than a majestic sweep of Dorset coastline. In the ▶ *high noon of Westcountry smuggling, this was a favourite rendezvous for the smugglers. Brandy and wines, silks and lace came ashore here and, under the cover of night, were moved swiftly inland – the smugglers knew the short cuts. Tales of 'ghosts' along the coastline and the country lanes were all part of the smugglers' strategy.*

BOSSINEY illustrator and author Felicity Young by the edge of the Atlantic on an October morning. I asked her why the sea has triggered so much ghostly manifestation. 'Maybe because it's this vast space untouched by humans ... the sea has these changing moods and strange qualities. I enjoy living by it ... the roar of the sea on some days, really thundering and these vivid colours. You have only to look at this coastline of North Cornwall to understand why we have had so many shipwrecks.' A keen horsewoman, Felicity has heard mysterious invisible hoofbeats in Trenale Lane, Tintagel at night.

44

THE SUPERNATURAL
AND THE SEA

IN THE FAR south west – Devon and Cornwall – we have coast-lines to both north and south. We have these magnificent edges to the sea, beautiful but cruel, wicked even in places. It is interesting to reflect much of our history, folklore superstition, and belief have all been fashioned by the sea: land once under water, echoes and speculation surrounding the lost land of Lyonesse – the sea is a natural breeding ground for strange stories and beliefs.

Our old Westcountry seamen were especially superstitious. In the days of sail, this awe was fully justified – vessels and men at the mercy of the thing we call chance in the shape of gales and storms. They believed no voyage should begin on certain days, on the last day of December, for example, when Judas is reputed to have hanged himself. Any Friday was regarded as a bad day for setting sail. They say Lord Byron deliberately flaunted this Friday theory by setting sail for Greece on a Friday – but Byron never made the return voyage. He died in Greece.

There is an even weirder Friday story. A certain group laid the keel of a vessel on a Friday, and named her after the day. They pushed their defiance further by launching her on that day, giving command to a captain called Friday and sent her on her maiden voyage on a Friday. The ship never reached port – and was never heard or seen of again.

As far as the supernatural goes, water does trigger a high percentage of manifestations. Springs, underground streams, wells, rivers and, of course, the sea often provide the setting of ghostly happening.

The phantom bells heard in St Ives Bay, the ghost ship seen in

45

the same majestic bay, the old man who haunts Frenchman's Creek, the black spectral ship in the bay near Porthcurno: Cornwall has many nautical echoes. And across the Tamar in Devon, there are strange claims about Sir Francis Drake and his famous drum.

Robert Stephen Hawker was vicar for 41 years at Morwenstow, where Cornwall ends and England begins. He became a legend in his life time, saving shipwrecked sailors on this notorious coastline and giving a decent Christian burial to those who perished.

On one dramatic occasion he was riding his pony Carrow from Welcombe back to Morwenstow and later recalled 'As I entered the gulph between the vallies today, a storm leaped from the sea, and rushed at me roaring – I recognised a demon and put Carrow into a gallop and so escaped.'

And travelling further up the other coastline we come to Dorset, another area soaked in smuggling tales and ghostly manifestation. The unmistakable figure of Napoleon Bonaparte, always with a companion, has been seen in Lulworth Cove. The French Emperor, in reality, never set foot on British soil, but in this brief time slip the great man turns away, folds his map – and vanishes into thin air. The supposition is he was looking for a suitable landing area for the French invasion of Britain.

The smugglers favoured the stretch of Chesil Beach to Burton Bradstock and Lyme Regis, and dominating the Dorset smuggling scene is Isaac Gulliver – not for nothing did they call him the King of the Dorset smugglers. When Gulliver mounted his last illicit operation in the 1700s, those 'in the know' observed an incredible two mile convoy of pack ponies led along the cliffs. Stories of 'ghost horses' heard at night travelling inland could generally be taken with a pinch of salt. Usually they were pack horses or ponies carrying smuggled goods.

The sea too has fired a rich creative harvest in words, music and paint. One of my favourite novels is *The Sea, The Sea* by Dame Iris Murdoch, first published back in 1978: a story set beside the sea, and a lonely and seemingly haunted house. Love and hate, fear and forgiveness all help to fashion a comic tragedy and a great novel.

Little wonder then the sea features so strongly in our supernatural kingdom.

To dream of the ocean can mean a variety of things: a good omen

A REMARKABLE sea coincidence took place in 1974. On the second day of September Sir Edward Heath, then Prime Minister, helped to publicise a novel by John Dyson entitled The Prime Minister's Boat Is Missing. *Five days later Sir Edward's yacht* Morning Cloud III *was lost at sea.*

if the sea is calm, a sign of mixed fortunes if choppy, and should the ocean be stormy then it is a warning that real courage will be needed to overcome obstacles.

They say Morgan Le Fay, Arthur's half-sister, had the power to raise phantom castles from the water and, of course, water is a recurring theme in the whole Arthurian tapestry: Arthur conceived at Tintagel within the sound of thunderous seas, five Arthurian battles fought on the shores of rivers, Arthur mortally wounded in battle alongside a river, his sword Excalibur returned to a water spirit, and finally the king borne away across water. All legend? Today more and more people believe in an Arthur. Some regard him as a military leader with a legendary reputation, like Sir Francis Drake on the high seas and more recently Field Marshal Viscount Montgomery in the desert.

Have we forgotten that historic triumph over the Spanish Armada? When the Spanish ships came up the Channel in 1588, witches on land with a great sense of patriotism, resolved to oppose them. Now when Queen Elizabeth later came to commemorate the defeat of the Spaniards, she had put on the medallions these words *'God blew with His winds and they were scattered.'* No mention of English gallantry at sea or Francis Drake. Clearly the fury of the wind seemed to the Queen the decisive factor. But this was no natural wind, for it drove the Spanish ships right round Scotland and the stragglers went back to Spain in disgrace. The important thing to remember is this fact: the old witches always had great powers over raising the winds. That is why no woman is supposed to whistle.

Mermaids are central characters in the folklore of the sea, but sane men on sea and land claim to have seen them. Henry Hudson, the explorer and navigator, made a matter-of-fact entry in his log concerning the sighting of a mermaid. Moreover, Hudson named the two seamen who saw the mermaid. An experienced seaman, he would hardly have bothered to record a hoax, or a piece of fiction.

There have, in fact, been some very precise details of sightings. As recently as December 1977 in South Africa *The Pretoria News* described 'a European woman from the waist up, whilst the rest of her body was shaped like the back end of a fish...'

TOM LETHBRIDGE
IN DEVON

THEY CALLED HIM 'the Einstein of the paranormal.' Tom Lethbridge, MA, FSA, was a gifted all-rounder: an archaeologist who became a master dowser and in the Westcountry we are proud of his Devon links. He progressed from finding hidden objects to exploring that timeless world beyond the thing we call death. Colin Wilson has said 'His was one of the most remarkable and original minds in parapsychology.'

In a sentence, he was a man ahead of his time.

Richard Church, reviewing Tom Lethbridge's book *Ghost and Ghoul,* declared 'Here is a new concept of the validity of a belief in the survival of personality after the death of the body. It makes the scepticism of the so-called rationalists look old-fashioned.'

It all began back in the early 1930s when Lethbridge and a fellow archaeologist were hunting the Viking graves on Lundy off the north coast of Devon. They found the graves and then proceeded to try experimenting with dowsing. Within the landscape of Lundy are seams of volcanic rock. Tom Lethbridge resolved to see if he could locate the seams that pass up through the slate. Cutting a hazel twig and being blindfolded, his friend then led him out onto the cliff path, the forked hazel twig held firmly in his hands. Whenever he passed directly over a volcanic seam, the hazel fork reacted violently. His colleague had a magnetometer and was therefore able to confirm Tom Lethbridge had truly located every volcanic seam.

To Lethbridge this all made sense. As with running water, a volcanic seam had a slight magnetic field.

In his book *Ghost & Divining Rod* he showed himself to be a truly

49

TOM Lethbridge in 1957.

master dowser. *Psychic News*, reviewing the book said,

'With an impressive weight of experimental evidence to back his view, this archaeologist/author believes the time is not far distant when scientists will be forced to recognise the dowser's divining twig as comparable in importance for the 21st century as the apple was in Newton's discovery of the laws of gravitation. His book abundantly testifies that man's sixth sense can tune in to a fabulous invisible world of interlocking force-fields.'

I know the reality of dowsing from some modest personal experience. Back in 1987 Don Wilkins, the celebrated Cornish dowser, gave me an interview at his home near Chacewater, and during that interview I had the privilege of sharing the stick with first Don and then his wife Margaret. At certain points, the stick was virtually pulled from my hand by some hidden power. The violent behaviour had nothing to do with any prompting from either Margaret or Don. Later, too, they allowed me to operate solo, and it was an extraordinary experience, the stick coming suddenly alive and almost taking the skin from my hands.

But there was more to T.C. Lethbridge than dowsing. Anyone wanting the complete philosophy of the man should read his books – they are mines of the supernatural. There are I think, eight volumes in all, including *Gogmagog, the Buried Gods, Witches, Investigating an Ancient Religion*, and concluding with *The Power of the Pendulum* which was published after his death.

In a number of them Mr Lethbridge explored the theory that there is a variety of field forces connecting woods and water, hills and open areas. He further suggested if this were so, it would account for previously seemingly baffling appearances, emotions and experiences.

In his chapter on Lethbridge in *The Ghost Hunters*, Peter Underwood perceptively reflected 'It may well be that the dowser and the ghost hunter should walk hand in hand, and that is what Tom Lethbridge frequently did.

'When Lethbridge's experiments into the pendulum and its reactions led him to believe that dowsing and psychometry – pictures of past events sparked off by touch – were linked, it seemed that he had stumbled upon something very important a new dimension of reality. He came to accept that the pendulum can be as accurate

51

as a voltmeter although there is no direct connection.'

Constantly experimenting and exploring, Tom Lethbridge in time came to believe that Nature is packed with strange tape recordings, dating back thousands and thousands of calendars.

He reached his 'tape recording' idea through personal experiences. When only a teenager he was out walking with his mother in some woodland near Wokingham; suddenly, at a certain point both mother and son felt extremely depressed. In a matter of just a few days the corpse of a suicide was found close to that particular spot.

It was Steven Shipp, who runs Midnight Books with his wife Frances, from Sidmouth, who reminded me Mr and Mrs Lethbridge came to live at Hole House, a Tudor mansion on the coast near Bromscombe in South Devon. They had left Cambridge disgusted by the hostile reception to one of Tom's books. It was an important move because in neighbouring Hole Mill lived a Devon 'wise woman'.

A woman of 'considerable and unusual faculties of extrasensory perception', Mrs N told Tom and Mina Lethbridge how she stopped unwanted visitors coming to Hole Mill. She drew a five pointed star in her head and then visualised the pentagram in the path of the unwanted man or woman.

One day Tom Lethbridge was looking down towards Hole Mill when he saw Mrs N emerge from her house – she looked up to Tom and waved in the distance – but he was puzzled by a strange second figure who appeared behind Mrs N. When they later discussed the second person, Mrs N said 'So you're seeing my ghosts now, are you?'

Interestingly on this occasion he was able to describe the colours worn by the phantom lady visitor whereas a year earlier in Cambridge it was the lack of colour that struck him.

On that earlier occasion as an undergraduate he had been leaving a friend's room when a man in a top hat appeared. Believing this life-like man to be a college porter with a message for his friend, he merely went out and said 'Good night'. The man did not speak. Next day, Tom Lethbridge asked his friend about the identity of the 'college porter'. His friend denied anybody had come with any message on the previous evening. When Tom Lethbridge really thought about it he realized the man had been wearing hunting attire. Then why had he not recognised the traditional red hunting coat? He now recalled it had been grey – like a black and white photograph. His friend's rooms overlooked the river.

To the subject of ghosts Tom Lethbridge brought the trained orderly mind of the scientist. His ultimate conclusions were this: ghosts are pictures rather than the spirits of departed men and women, children and animals.

Here I will make just one small personal point. On a November afternoon in 1984 I saw a cyclist travelling on the Bodmin to Camelford road in North Cornwall. He and his cycle disappeared suddenly, defying all logical explanation. Interestingly the man and

HOLE HOUSE, near Branscombe, in South Devon, where Tom and Mina Lethbridge lived during their Westcountry years. He made use of the long stairwell at Hole House for his pendulum dating notions. Steven Shipp, the supernatural bookseller, on a recent visit to the property described it as 'extremely peaceful.'

the machine were greyish, no other distinct colour, rather like an old photograph in a family album and, on reflection, he was wearing clothes of an earlier period. Maybe I had seen something in Cornwall like Tom Lethbridge had seen in Cambridge in 1922.

As for Tom Lethbridge's time in South Devon, his neighbour's death led to another important experience. Walking past her cottage, he experienced an unpleasant feeling, a suffocating sense of depression. Following his natural curiosity, he walked around the cottage, and in doing so made a significant discovery. He was able to walk into and then out of the depression.

As a boy I enjoyed seeing how a magnet would suddenly seize a nail or a pin. Even then it struck me there must be some kind of unseen boundary, and perhaps there is a similar unseen boundary in the supernatural field.

Tom Lethbridge made other interesting experiments locally. In the garden of the South Devon house there were archaeological remains and by dangling the pendulum over an ancient skull he was able to determine that it was a man's skull. If, for instance, the pendulum swung around in a circular movement then it was a female. If however it swung back and forth it was male. He also went into the courtyard at Hole House and dowsed for pieces of pottery. While at Blackbury Castle he used his pendulum as the method of dating sling shots.

Another episode happened on a winter's morning when Tom and Mina Lethbridge went down to Ladram Bay to collect some seaweed. Tom felt an air of depression as he filled the sacks. Mina, who had walked across the beach, hurried back saying 'Let's go. I can't stand this place a minute longer...'

There were other visits to Ladram beach, other depressions. Nine years after that first depression on the seaweed expedition, a man committed suicide there.

Always water.

Thomas Charles Lethbridge was a psychic explorer par excellence.

I wonder if his ghost is ever seen or felt in the Branscombe area. We can be sure of this: if the quest continues on the other side then Tom Lethbridge will be exploring, searching for the answer – or answers.

THE KEY, in many cases, Tom Lethbridge believed, was water. As an archaeologist, he was always interested in dowsing and water divining; a real all-rounder in fact. He also noted how strange things often happened in warm damp conditions.

Let the man himself have the last say. In 1965 his book *ESP, Beyond Time & Distance* appeared and he concluded it with these words from South Devon:

'There I will leave this story and return while I may to the three-dimensional world with the green of the grass and the far off grumble of the sea on the pebble beach; to the buzzards wheeling over the combe and the gulls shouting to each other. All have life in them today in three dimensions; but it is becoming clear that although this life may apparently die, yet it remains alive in a fourth. Perhaps I have really seen the green ray after all and been too occupied with trivialities to appreciate what I was looking at. Yes, of course this must be the case, for this morning just as I was finishing this book, I saw the swallows come. At one moment there was no swallow to be seen anywhere. Suddenly some tiny specks swept in from the sea. They raced over the roof of the shed where last year's nests are still on the rafters, passing over the ancient cider apple-tree, which is almost completely hollow and full of water. And then, for an instant, they hung in the air fluttering. They swung round in a swift arc and swooped through the half-door into the shed. They had passed the end of their ray, which stretched from here across Africa, and for a second did not know what had happened. Then they realized that they were home.'

ANOTHER KIND OF WRITING – AND ANIMAL WELFARE

WRITING in a trance-like condition became the fashion in the late 1700s. Even in those pre-Freud times, it was generally accepted that the bulk of this written material came from the author's unconscious mind. Not all, though, accepted that view: some claimed such work was dictated by authors in the spirit world, an outstanding example being *The Pilgrimage of Thomas Pains* by C. Hammond in which a prominent agnostic described his experiences after death.

Even more impressive was a whole sequence of automatic writings received by a group of well-educated women at the turn of the century, only one of whom was a professional medium. The material seems to have come from three men who had died, all well-known psychical researchers in their early lives: F.W.H. Myers, who wrote *The Human Personality and its Survival After Death*, Edmund Gurney, a Fellow of Trinity College, Cambridge, who checked many case histories and did valuable work on hypnosis and other paranormal subjects, and Henry Sidgwick, another Fellow of Trinity, a man of great integrity, who was President of the Society for Psychical Research.

That is all background, but back in 1987, I resolved to meet a present day 'other kind of writer' and Claire Wolferstan, who lives near Weston-Super-Mare, was recommended as a genuine lady – and fine example of this psychic craft. She and her husband James came to see me in North Cornwall, and we had a fascinating three hour meeting. Since then we have gone on corresponding and discussing such writing and allied subjects.

An important development in her life was her former marriage to

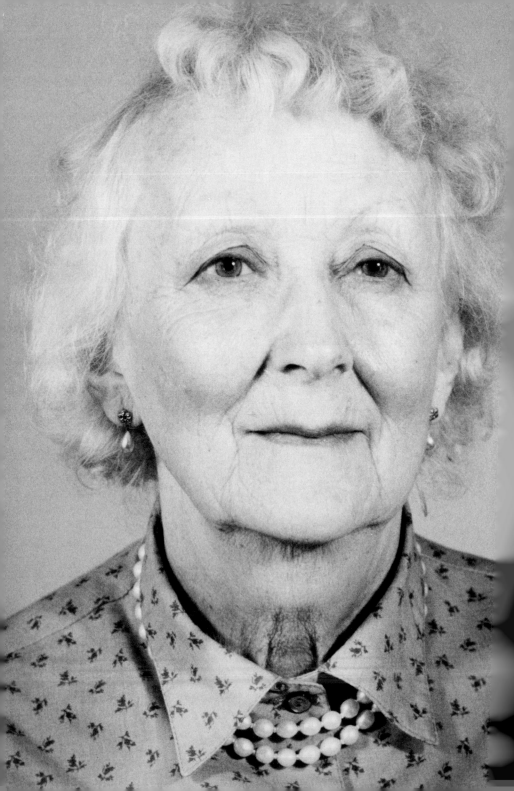

William Mitchell, a man fascinated by communication between this world and the next.

'We formed a weekly circle,' Claire told me, 'in order to pray for healing. Added to this, my husband became extremely interested in automatic writing and he made a gadget out of hardboard shaped like Concorde with a small hole cut in it to hold a pen or pencil. This we placed on a large drawing block and having first, as always, prayed to God for protection from any harmful or malicious entities – and I must stress the importance of this precaution – we invited any discarnate being to write as we placed our hands on the board. Vague sloping lines came at first as from someone who wrote in italics, and then came "John Mitchell", rather sprawlingly, my husband's late father, and later still "Jack Mitchell" my husband's elder brother who had died recently. It seemed too good to be true.

'The next development was when a friend said: "Try holding the pen yourself!" and lo! it worked, Jack writing through me in his handwriting, also sloping and quite unlike my own. This was terribly exciting, and very soon he wrote: "Do not only write on Thursday (the day of our meetings) but practice in between."

'This I did and then to my amazement I was told I was to write a book under the auspices of no less a person than St John the Baptist. This I did, and different discarnate personalities were sent to dictate a chapter to me, dealing with the subject on which they had been expert during life and of course they continue their studies in the afterlife. So a geologist gave me his chapter, Mesmer his on hypnosis and so on. The book is called *Message to Mankind* by Margaret Claire Mitchell, as I then was. It was a most moving experience taking it down, particularly as my husband, towards the end of it, was dying of lung cancer and life was unbearable.

◀ *CLAIRE WOLFERSTAN who lives at Worle near Weston-Super-Mare, is 'another kind of writer.' 'I'm a Scorpio,' she told me. 'Aren't Scorpios always supposed to be drawn to the Occult and the solving of mysteries. Well, this one is …'*

'It was published at the end of 1974. Before I finished it I found I was hearing the words in my mind, as indeed I do now, and I remember Jack saying to me, rather sadly it seemed, "Oh Claire you don't need me any more."

"Please don't leave me!" I think I said, as I clung to these new relationships in my misery. Nor have they left me. I can contact them mentally whenever I want, and also the Mighty Entity with whom I now converse and who will expatiate to me on any subject I ask, or you or anybody else asks. I believe the only limitations to be the vocabulary stored in my mind. So I would be no use taking down technicalities on say, engineering or chemical formulae.'

More recently she has published *Unknown Peoples of this Planet* with a foreword by Sir George Trevelyan: again a kind of literary telepathy between Claire and 'a discarnate being'.

As a member of the International League for the Protection of Horses and the RSPCA, I have a special interest in animal welfare. I was heavily involved in the campaign to stop the export of live equines for the dinner table in Europe – a campaign brilliantly spearheaded by ILPH – and remain deeply concerned about the live export of all food animals on these long unnecessary journeys to other countries.

Claire Wolferstan knows all this, and consequently sent me thoughts entitled *The Role of the Animal Kingdom on Earth* for this book. 'But,' she stressed, 'Michael, will you make it clear that it's not automatic writing? It was only at the outset back in 1973 ... I very soon learnt to "hear" the dictation in my inner mind; so it's telepathy between the third and fourth dimensions.'

The following then are words she has received from 'out there':

The Role Of The Animal Kingdom On Earth

'Until recently it was generally assumed that the animal kingdom was to be considered as subordinate to man and to be "fair game" for him, whether as food, or for hunting, as draught animals, domestic pets, for use in clothing and in medical research. In all these aspects little or no consideration has been given to the welfare of the animal, whether for its physical well being or for its soul's evolution, and this is entirely due to the powerful influence the force of evil has had on the minds of incarnate man, and which is only now beginning to wane.

ANIMALS are the charges of mankind, to whom they should be able to look for protection ...

'The only way to enlighten man as to the correct way to approach the subject of the animal kingdom on Earth is by regarding them as the charges of mankind to whom they should be able to look for protection and support during their life span, for they too have been obliged to manifest under far harsher conditions than was originally intended by God.

'This again was due to the disobedience of Satanaku set in charge of Earth when it was first ordained that it should support life; and when he lowered the rate of vibration on which both man and beast were to manifest, thereby causing them to suffer the privations and hazards concommitant with physical life on Earth.

'Certain highly evolved beings now incarnate on Earth are well aware that animals should have received very different treatment than that to which they have been subjected in the past, and they have devoted their lives to succouring them and upholding their cause in every way possible; but world opinion is in general apathetic, and too lethargic to demand action from the relevant authorities for any large scale improvement to be made in their lot. Only

61

when public demand is such that governments and local authorities feel obliged to accede to their demands, will the necessary action be taken to ensure that the animal kingdom receives the treatment which God has ordained for it.

'With regard to those species threatened with extinction it should be recognised that certain species of life on Earth be they insect, fish or mammal have served that purpose for which they came to Earth and therefore it is of little use lamenting their departure; rather devote your energies to the care of those species which have been abused by mankind and which have suffered hardship, fear, pain and degradation as a result. Those species of life now manifesting on Earth which are known to be harmful to both man and beast, or to the crops on which they live such as the tetse fly, locusts and similar pests should not only be allowed to become extinct but should be encouraged to do so, as should all venomous species be they bacteria or poisonous insects or snakes for these are not of God's creation. They were introduced by the force of evil, or else had been altered from His original conception by this same force, in order to cause suffering and distress to those creatures of God's creation on Earth. So let us not be sentimental over those forms of life which destroy or cause disease to the natural fauna on this planet. Wherever there is a chance of any such species be it virus, reptile, fish or animal becoming extinct in the foreseeable future, have no hesitation whatsoever in allowing them to do so, for these species are alien to this planet and have no place in its scheme of life. You may first photograph them, analyse them in every respect, record their behavioural patterns, set them up in museums, write text books about them, bottle them, but do not become obsessed by the need for their preservation.

'Here is a clear case for getting priorities right, and it should be recognised that the plight of man or beast, and the crops which form their food supplies, is of greater importance than the plight of intruders on this planet whose introduction in the first place was solely in order to aggravate the harsh lot of all living creatures sent by God to manifest on Earth.

'Once it has been established that the animal kingdom should share equal rights with man it will be recognised that they should no longer be used for the following purposes: food, clothing, haulage, and above all the despicable practice of using them for medical research would be banned. This last it could be claimed has proved of great benefit to mankind, but in point of fact it has been common knowledge in the relevant circles that the use of animals was not necessary in the field of research where other techniques have already been evolved; and that it is only due to a reluctance on the part of those in charge of the laboratories to change their customary methods that this change has not come about already.

'This reluctance is inexcusable for these research workers know full well in their hearts that the animals in their care, even if not actually suffering pain, are leading miserable and totally unnatural lives. If the full facts were revealed to the general public the outcry would be such that the practice of experimentation on live animals would be stopped immediately.

'Lastly it should be borne in mind that animals are of a different order to that of mankind, so that although they are manifesting on the same plane of existence as human beings and are subject to the same physical laws yet nevertheless they are less highly evolved and altogether younger in terms of human reference and should never be regarded as being on a par with human intelligence, nor should they be taught to respond to human situations in a manner unnatural to their species, as for example putting their talents on display before an audience. Not only are they being made to behave in a manner unnatural to their kind, but they are also responding to the electrical vibration on which their audience operates and this raises them to a higher vibration than that on which they should by rights be operating. This will render them restless when they are with their own kind, and filled with vague longings which they are incapable of understanding when they are in human company, and these sensations of belonging neither to the animal world nor the human is detrimental to the creature's welfare.

'The psychic powers of animals are considerable as has often been remarked by human beings, and here again these are more in evidence when they are left in their natural state for they will then be more attuned to those spirit entities whom God has set in charge of them, and who influence their minds in order to maintain

ARE animals more receptive than humans to psychic phenomena? There are many tales which would seem to bear out this belief.

their life's cycle in such matters as migration, mating, the food they should eat, and the food they should avoid, and in fact in all matters relating to their physical welfare. It is true that very often animals become aware of what are commonly termed 'ghosts' whether animal or human, and here again it is generally due to an unnaturally close association with the world of humans that they have been made aware of the fourth dimension and usually this fills them with a sense of disquiet and unease for they know instinctively that they do not belong to that dimension.'

Post Script:

'Since mankind has been obliged to live his earthly life in a manner wholly unacceptable to God due entirely to the workings of the force of evil, he has turned to the animal kingdom for comfort and companionship in many instances throughout time, and where this reliance on the part of man on God's lowlier creation would be deplored had all gone as He ordained, as conditions are the situation is altogether different. The lifestyle imposed on man through the ages renders him vulnerable in many respects, for he finds himself in a hostile environment quite unlike that from which he came during the interval between earth lives in what he generally termed heaven, for not only is it liable to be harsh climatically, but in the struggle to survive life tends to be 'every man for himself.'

'Thus it will be seen that the individual may often find him or herself isolated from human friends due to various unfortunate circumstances, and it is then that they may turn to the animal kingdom for comfort and consolation. This tendency is a subconscious realisation that they are in need of the love of God, and that this love is being channelled to them through His lesser creatures where it should by rights have reached them through their own kind. This deviation from God's plan is recognised by Him as being the lesser evil, for He would not have any one of His dear children live lonely and unloved lives since He is well aware that life without love is desolation indeed.'

GHOSTLY FEMALES

AT THE OUTSET of my supernatural investigations back in the mid 60s, one thing struck me: the number of ghostly females greatly outnumbers phantom men. Then I discovered an interesting fact: there are fewer men in Britain, and always have been, so for once the paranormal pattern is the logical.

But we would be wrong to assume all are nuns and unhappy lovers. Truth is there is an incredibly wide range of ghostly females. There have been barmaids and aristocrats, pregnant girls and elderly spinsters – even a highwaywoman. Interestingly too they have been seen in all sorts of settings, multi-storey carparks and club houses on golf courses, ancient monasteries and castles and a phone box!

Chapel Street, Penzance, is one of the really historic streets of Cornwall, and boasts a curious lady ghost. Mrs Elizabeth Baines owned a small orchard hereabouts, and did not like the idea of people stealing her fruit. As a result she employed a local fisherman to act as guard and provided him with a pistol. One evening, nearing harvest time, Mrs Baines went to the orchard to check her guard was doing his job. He was indeed – to such an extent that not recognising her and sensing she was a thief, he opened fire and killed her! The ghost of Mrs Baines in dark cloak and bonnet has been seen near the top of the street where she disappears through a solid wall.

◀ *GHOSTLY females abound in all sorts of settings – even in a phone box.*

Our celebrated local ghost here on the edge of Bodmin Moor is Charlotte Dymond who was murdered by her jealous lover on a Sunday in April 1844. Charlotte has been seen walking in that area below Roughtor, notably by sentries of the Old Volunteers who were so convinced she haunted the place that officers had difficulty in getting men to stand on sentry duty. Moreover Charlotte is no vague ghostly figure because there have been precise descriptions of the clothes she wears: a gown of various colours, a red cloth shawl and silk bonnet. I have never seen her, but our terrier Tex behaved very oddly and out of character early one morning on the slopes and summit of Roughtor. Did he see Charlotte?

Across the Tamar in Devon, High street, Exeter, is another historic thoroughfare. *The Exeter Express* in February 1973 published an interesting story. Peter Rouse, manager of a clothes shop in the street, went to the store below the sale room to check stock. Mr Rouse was puzzled to find clothing swinging on the racks which suggested some person might be hiding among the garments. He called a colleague and together they investigated. They saw the head of a girl gliding towards them – but no ordinary girl for suddenly she vanished into thin air. Later Gillian Davis, a shop assistant, saw the same ghostly girl in the same area of the building. Once more the phantom vanished when only a matter of feet from Miss Davis.

I am puzzled by the fact that there have never been reported sightings on Dartmoor of Kitty Jay's ghost. The life of Kitty Jay was a tragedy from beginning to end, and even in death she remains a Dartmoor mystery.

Kitty was born an orphan in the 18th century. She was sent to work on a farm on the Moor. There she was seduced by a farmer's son and then rejected. Carrying his child, she hanged herself in a barn, seeing no other solution to her problems.

No suicide could be buried on consecrated land. So the first available crossroads became her burial place. In those superstitious days suicides were regarded as potential vampires who might 'walk'.

You'll find her grave set back from the road above Manaton, between Heatree Cross and Swallerton Gate: a grassy mound with a raised foot and headstone.

Mystery deepens in that Kitty's grave is never minus fresh flow-
·ers. I have journeyed past the grave dozens of times and have
never found it otherwise. Furthermore you cannot get a local person to 'name' the provider of these floral tributes to Kitty.

Odd too are the sightings of a ghostly man by her grave. The
farmer's son perhaps?

Somerset is well populated by phantom ladies, and they are
extraordinary for their diversity. The old prison at Shepton Mallet,
which was an infamous Army 'glasshouse' until 1966, is reputed to
have 'a white lady' who was beheaded there in 1680. There have
been various accounts of phantom white ladies standing guard over
Somerset bridges and trackways, and at Crowcombe Rectory 'a
lady in blue' has been seen, apparently harmless, identity
unknown.

Does Arthur belong to reality or legend? The debate continues.
Though more and more people are coming to see Arthur as an historical probability. Interesting then that a radiant female phantom
has been seen in the vicinity of Glastonbury Tor. Some say she is
Guinevere and they may be right, for there is the tale of an excava-
tion at Glastonbury in the 1100s and the discovery of the skeleton
of a lady with long strands of golden hair still clinging to her skull.
That golden hair turned to dust when exposed to the air, and those
golden tresses are reputed to be the source of the strange light in
which her ghostly form is bathed.

◀ *SOME say she may be Guinevere ...*

THE spectre of a woman in a long white costume ... ▶

Dorset too has more than her fair share of such manifestations. The lady dressed in grey, 'always wearing a grey cap' who haunted the former preparatory school at Charlton Marshall, and the various ghosts of Athelhampton Hall, Puddletown, including yet another female in grey. The ghost of Lillie Langtry, beautiful mistress of King Edward VII, at Bournemouth, and the strange lady of the River Stour who has been seen at different locations near Longham.

The number of ghosts in grey compel the question: 'Why that colour?'

I put that question, a while back, to Acora, the Romany clairvoyant, and he said 'Grey's a very lucky colour for many people.'

I put the same question to someone who knows a good deal about psychology, and he explained: 'Grey should be the dominant colour worn by a man or woman wanting to convince others or to be accepted by an audience.'

But maybe neither answer gets to the heart of this ghostly matter. Could it be that ghosts are possibly half in this world and half in the next – a grey area?

Nuns too frequently appear in hauntings. I'm not sure why, but a keen student of superstition told me seeing nuns in the here and now can be a good or bad omen. Apparently to meet one or more is a good sign, provided you avoid looking at their backs when they have passed!

Now on to Wiltshire, the beginning and the end of Bosinney publishing territory. Once more we find ourselves in fertile ghost hunting country. At Maddington in 1970 Mr Alexander of Shrewton and his daughter were working in a barn. They both saw the spectre – a young woman in a long white costume – who inexplicably vanished. But both remembered the distinct footsteps and the rustle of her long white costume. They had no doubts: they had seen a ghost.

David Foot in his perceptive introduction to *Wiltshire Mysteries* has written 'Like no other county, Wiltshire creaks, groans and intrigues with its inexhaustible reserves of history. Every hamlet has a story to tell. Every country house supposedly has its ghost...'

Mr Foot is correct and beautiful Longleat personifies those very qualities. They say the second Lord Weymouth killed his wife's lover and buried him. Years later when central heating was installed, the badly decomposed body of a young man was found under old flagstones in the cellar.

A passage on the top floor has long been known as 'The Green Lady's Walk.' A portrait of the beautiful Louisa in the house shows her dressed in green.

But there are other parts of Longleat and other ghosts. Peter Underwood, President of the Ghost Club, has done a fascinating section on the house in our *Wiltshire Mysteries*. I mention them here not only to sustain the female theme but to show some ghosts have very vivid colours.

The sound of light footsteps and the rustle of a silken gown descending the oak staircase at Throop Hall; Erlestoke House, now a detention centre, is reputedly haunted by a lady in green, known as Lady Charlotte; at Lydiard Millicent the ghost of Sir Ferdinando Blunt's wife haunts the garden of the manor house where she witnessed the murder of her lover. Wiltshire is full of ghostly sights and echoes.

Unfortunately I have never seen a phantom lady – but then can I be sure? That girl who walked down the narrow lane past our cottage last evening did not reply. Who was she? That elderly lady crossing the road the other morning in Wadebridge. She seemed to disappear from sight rather suddenly. In the supernatural field you soon discover seeing is not always believing.

But I have often heard the ghostly footsteps of a young girl in our days at Bossinney – and Sonia heard them too.

Yes, at the very edge of the unknown.

A PHANTOM *black dog has been seen on this road high above Bossiney. This area of North Cornwall has triggered an exceptional range of manifestations: ghostly monks and invisible footsteps and hoofbeats, invisible mocking laughter – and a good deal else. Why? It is an inevitable but, at present, unanswerable question. Maybe one day we shall get the answer or answers. I have a strong feeling the 21st century will produce a frontier where science will meet the paranormal.*

ANIMAL
EXPERIENCES

THE BEAST OF EXMOOR has not only been widening his territory, he has been haunting Bossiney publishing since 1985 when we produced *Westcountry Mysteries*, introduced by Colin Wilson.

In that now out of print title, Jillian Powell contributed a fine in-depth chapter on the mysterious creature who had been terrorising farm animals in North Devon and Somerset.

Then in the summer of 1993 Ronnie Hoyle in his *Strange Tales of the South West* updated the continuing saga, showing this strange four-legged terror was more recently making his more devilish attacks in Cornwall. The odd thing is the Beast has not been caught, not shot, not even photographed.

Anyway, he was far from my thoughts as I was driving to Jamaica Inn on book business one morning. My thoughts were miles away from the supernatural when I had this unusual experience – so unusual that the next evening dining with Peter Underwood, the then President of the Ghost Club, I related the episode. The Ghost Club is interested in all matters mysterious – and Peter suggested I should submit a report. The following is just that:

'On Wednesday 19th May 1993 I was driving towards the village of St Breward on the edge of Bodmin Moor. It was in the region of 9.30 am and as I passed a roadside cottage, a black animal crossed the road in front of the car about 15 yards ahead. At first I thought it was a fox but then realized the very black colour was akin a cat or dog. It was too large for a cat, and did not have the look of a dog in that it moved with its body very low to the ground, as a cat does when it is hunting. It disappeared into woods on my right having appeared from the other side of the road.

'On reflection, it looked more like a puma than any other kind of animal. Having published drawings of the beast of Exmoor, I felt certain it was closely related to that strange animal which has been seen but never caught over a wide area of Exmoor, Devon and even here in Cornwall.

'On the following afternoon I called on the owner of the roadside cottage, and asked if she or anyone locally owned a large black dog, but she assured me nobody in that area owned such a dog. I explained details of the sighting, and her view was the animal could have been the one responsible for mysterious sheep killings on the moor.

'That evening, my former secretary Linda Turner, on hearing my account, said she had seen this same strange animal near her home just outside St Breward.

'Report for The Ghost Club, 25 May 1993.'

In the paranormal field cats have had a rather mixed press. Some have seen the cat as a fiendish agent of the Devil himself. Others claimed cats have been worshipped as gods. The cat certainly features prominently in the realm of superstition. Black cats are reputed to be lucky; if one runs across our path, the Romanies advise us to put a wish on the animal, and here in the Westcountry there have been well-documented cases of ghostly cats.

What does it all mean? Do these ghostly cat appearances mean animals go beyond the thing we call death? As an animal lover I would like to think so. If death really is the end of the road for us all, then how do we account for ghosts?

All of which leads us on to another important feline question. Are cats psychic?

Back in 1986 I had an interesting experience at the Bush Inn, Morwenstow, recording a programme for BBC Radio Cornwall for a series entitled *Ghost Hunt*.' Now the Bush has a genuinely haunted reputation, and though we did not see a ghost we certainly picked up strange sounds which defied all logical explanation. There were four of us in this small upstairs room which had suddenly gone colder – four of us plus a cat.

At one point in the recorded interview I said '…the most interesting incident so far has been at the attitude of the cat. Now cats

MORE *and more people are coming to the view that cats often see things which are invisible to human beings. Cats feature significantly in our remembered dreams: their behaviour varies, and depending on their behaviour lies the prophetic quality of the dream. Historically too cats were the companions of witches. Cats can also show a remarkable appreciation of music. Jehanne Jean-Charles in her* Book of Cats *told how a kitten of hers went mad about a Vivaldi record – so much so that the animal discovered by putting the pick-up back to the start, it could hear the music all over again.*

are very psychic animals, and he was giving the very definite impression that he knows we are expecting something to happen, or someone to arrive ... I feel he's got that air of anticipation.'

And Jim Gregory, the landlord, commented. 'The cat very definitely, as you said, has an air of anticipation; but also he actually moved towards the north wall, and look at him now. He is in the pointing position. He's looking at this wall here. Now that's the wall from which the noises come.'

I agreed, adding 'It may be his mechanism is picking up something that we're not. I certainly, in personal experiences, have found that animals are often a more valuable witness, a more reliable one than human beings.'

One man, who believed cats had psychic powers, was Nicholas Kendall, a former High Sheriff of Cornwall, who lived for many years in the family home Pelyn, on top of the hill outside Lostwithiel. We came to know one another through RSPCA work, and he believed his cats often picked up presences unseen to human beings. Nick told me his cats had, on occasions, stared at an invisible something with such intensity he was convinced they were, in reality, seeing something or someone beyond ordinary human vision – and on occasions he would see two of his cats staring in the same direction, at the same spot – a kind of double confirmation, and his wife Frances agreed.

Cats frequently feature in our dreams.

Julia and Derek Parker in their magnificent book *Dreaming*, published by Mitchell Beazley back in 1985, had this to say on the subject of cats in dream experiences:

'To many people there can be something mysterious and even slightly uncanny about a cat (after all, they were traditional companions of witches). But they are also highly sensual creatures: could the cat in the dream represent a beautiful object of desire? Was it purring and contented? Were you fondling it? If it was showing its claws and snarling perhaps your unconscious is suggesting that you should be more assertive in waking life. Or perhaps it was a criticism – have you been "catty" recently?'

As someone, who dreams every night *and* cares about equine welfare, I was interested to hear of a very vivid horse racing dream by John Godley, later Lord Kilbracken. It was, in fact, a double

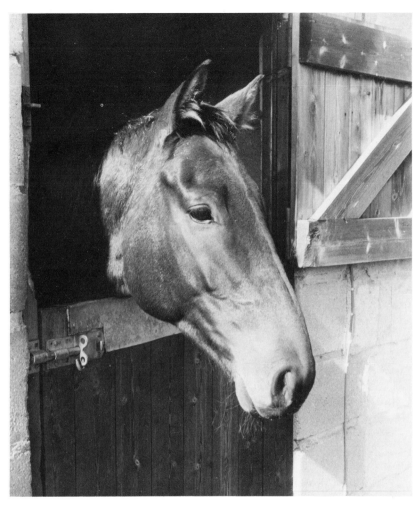

AS SOMEONE who is actively involved in equine animal welfare, I am fascinated by the number of ghost horses, ponies and donkeys relating to the Westcountry. Does this mean equines go on beyond the thing we call death? There is no doubt horses can and do show extraordinary sensitivity. Patrizia Krachmalnicoff in her book The Magic of Animals referred to horses having 'an interior life of their own, quite independently from any education that has been given them and which manifests itself in spontaneous, unexpected and absolutely human ways'.

79

dream experience. First, John Godley 'saw' a horse carrying the colours of the Gaekwar of Baroda gain an impressive victory, and in the next race he heard the crowd shouting for the favourite, a horse called Bogie. Unfortunately he then woke up – and did not 'see' the outcome of the second race.

Next day John Godley turned to the racing page of his newspaper, and discovered a horse owned by the Gaekwar of Baroda, called Baroda Squadron, was running that afternoon. In the next race, the favourite was a runner named The Brogue.

Mr Godley backed his dreams and put money on both horses. He also told friends about his dream and his wager. In fact he committed to paper a statement about his forecasts, dated and witnessed by three individuals. He took the envelope to his local post office where it was sealed and stamped with the official time stamp and locked in the post office safe.

Both horses won.

The really great race horse trainers and jockeys, men like Henry Cecil and Lester Piggott, have a natural empathy with horses, almost a sixth sense. And what of horses themselves? I have a hunch they are often highly sensitive and perceptive. Here is an interesting story from Peter Thomas, an old cricketing friend and retired farmer from St-Just-in-Penwith.

'Major and Prince were both born on the farm and Bill, my brother, and I grew up with them. We were unharnessing them at lunch time in a field at the top of Truthwall Lane. Suddenly they both wheeled round to face down the lane towards the sea. They were both absolutely rigid and held their heads high as if looking at some distant object. Bill and I both looked in this direction but could see and hear nothing. After at least half a minute a mini whirlwind struck the gorse on the hedge not five yards from us. It lasted several seconds with bits of the bush flying into the air – then it was gone. There were portions of the bush stripped bare. Major and Prince just relaxed and we went to lunch having witnessed at first hand how animals, even domesticated animals, are one up on us humans.'

DREAMS RECALLED
IN VIVID DETAIL

DOWN THE AGES dreams have fascinated men and women. In our dreams, fragments of reality are transformed – sometimes distorted – combining almost to produce a kind of theatre. The old people believed dreams were messages from the gods. A more modern interpretation is they are keys to the unconscious.

Here are four dreams recalled by Jack Benney, a Cornishman and keen student of the supernatural, who lives at Penwartha near Perranporth. He told me 'They started shortly after I had an operation in 1970. There were four, the last about 1975. It was as if while asleep my spirit had left the sleeping body and had gone on a journey into the unknown. I don't think my subconscious would have conjured up such dreams in vivid detail. If these dreams had occurred in Old Testament days they would have been looked upon as visions.'

First Dream

'I want you to imagine a pitch dark night on a wild moor. A gale is blowing and the rain is coming down in torrents. I am battling against the elements and thorns and brambles are tearing at my face and clothes, when suddenly, in front of me, a very steep and narrow stairway appeared. There seemed to be sides extending up the stairs to the ceiling. A landing ran across the top like a letter 'T'. There was a wall, the whole width of the landing and reaching to the ceiling, on this wall, facing the stairs, was a shelf about four inches wide and four feet in length, which I could just reach with my fingertips if I stood on my toes. From somewhere overhead a light lit up the stairs.

'On the left of the landing was an alcove or recess in which there was a stone bench seat whereon sat a hideous and repulsive looking old man who had his legs sticking out straight in front of him with a crooked stick between them. The handle was between his feet and he held the bottom of the stick between his hands. He appeared to be muttering away to himself and drooling. He did not look at me as I came up the stairs from off the wild moor with the wind blowing up the stairway with a loud roar. As I walked upwards I was carrying a woolly toy, a lamb, soft, white, and cuddly, the sort you would give to a young child. The whole reason I was there seemed that my mission was to stand the lamb on the shelf.

'This I attempted to do. I stood on my toes and reached up and was about to stand the lamb on the shelf when the old man, who before took no notice of me, reached out with his stick and hooked the turned handle around my ankle and gave a sharp pull which put me off balance just when I had about managed to stand the toy on the shelf. This caused the lamb to overbalance on to the landing from where it rolled off and down over each stair and out into the night from whence came the sound of demonic laughter somewhere out on the wild and dark moor.

'Down the stairs I went out into the night. I do not recall anything until I arrived back again at the stairway. This time there was the sound of many voices in pursuit, and the old man came down the stairs to meet me, cursing. With his stick he beat me about the head and body as hard as he could, while clustered around the foot of the stairs were a crowd of demons shouting and screaming with glee, although they made no attempt to climb the stairs after me. This time I was carrying an ornament, a white dove. After a great struggle I got this on to the shelf but again, like the lamb, the ornament fell to the landing where it broke into pieces, much to the delight of the demons – if that they were – whereupon the old man resumed his place in the alcove as before.

◀ *CARL Gustav Jung, born 1875, died 1961, believed in the idea of 'our active imagination': a technique of conscious dreaming in which we release the image-making powers of our unconscious minds.*

'Once more I turned and descended the stairs and went out into the night. Once again I remember nothing about the interval whilst out on the moor. Yet again I arrived back at the stairway, this time carrying a very large book like a family Bible. The binding was broken and therefore it was a mass of loose pages between the stiff covers. This time the demons were in hot pursuit and in greater numbers while the old man came down the stairs with renewed strength and fury cursing yet again, and beating me about the head and body. Again the demons were content to remain at the foot of the stairs, mouthing threats and slobbering away to each other. After a great struggle I managed to place the book on the high narrow shelf but it went sliding off and all the loose pages fluttered down the stairs, blown around like leaves by the wind which roared up the stairway. As the pages reached the bottom they were seized by the demons who tore them into shreds with their hands and teeth, all the time jumping up and down like demented apes but I managed to hold on to one page, which after a further struggle I at last placed on the shelf.

'I had no sooner done so, when the old man gave a shriek, either of rage or despair, ran across the landing and jumped down the shaft. Immediately a blinding flash of white light lit up the whole area and when I turned to walk down the stairway sunlight streamed up the stairs and when I reached the bottom, instead of a wild moorland scene, there in its place was a beautiful garden as far as could be seen, with people strolling around the numerous paths, with their arms around each other and looking very happy. It was then I awoke to this unhappy and violent world, and sad I was to do so.

'I am sure this dream or vision was to test me so that I might overcome the forces of evil, namely the black night, the demons and the evil looking old man, depicting the power of darkness. The toy lamb and the dove were symbols of purity and love, the book of loose pages so easily lost, was the book of knowledge and the final victory of attainment depicted by gaining the gateway to a higher existence by way of the shelf which opened the door to the beautiful scenery described.

Second Dream

'Instead of a wild moorland scene this one started half way up a mountain side, one of those remote, barren and rocky areas of this planet, with huge boulders strewn all over the mountain.

'My dream began on a very narrow and rocky path which was hardly seen, weaving upwards between the boulders and the rock-face of the mountain. The other path was a little wider, less stony and forked off to the right, leading downwards. On the left – hand side of this path the rock face rose sheer for hundreds of feet, rent by huge cracks in its surface, out of which issued vapours of smoke and fog. These vapours were also rising from the right-hand side. The further I travelled down the path the thicker they became; in the lower depths tongues of flame were to be seen and in addition there was the screaming and wailing of many voices.

'I had now reached a great arch of rock which spanned the path and it was here I halted with the instant feeling that once I had passed under this rock there would be no chance of turning back the way I had come. In other words, I had travelled the downward path far enough. A voice seemed to say, "Return to the place from whence you came" and immediately I found myself back on the stony upward path where I had started my dream.

'I now started to climb upwards to reach the summit of the mountain. This path was ten times harder to climb than the downward path had been, for every three steps upwards I slipped back two. At times I had to squeeze between huge boulders and the rock face, all the time slowly gaining ground. As I climbed higher the path became a little wider and less steep, then a strip of green appeared near the summit. This seemed to spread outwards like a triangle and when I finally reached the top of the mountain, there spread out before my eyes, was the most beautiful scene I ever saw.

'As far as I could see in every direction it was like a vast park, full of flowers and trees with paths going everywhere. On these paths people were walking about arm in arm, talking and laughing and looking very happy. Someone looked up and saw me and ran towards me with their hands outstretched as if to welcome me, but before I could recognise who it may have been I woke up and, once again, was sorry to do so.

'The ending was much like the first dream with its beautiful and peaceful atmosphere, lovely music and the songs of the many birds who were unafraid of humans.'

Third Dream

'In March 1975, my first cousin, Robert Mannel, the eldest son of Rosina Mannel (nee Benney) died of cancer. Bob was one of the best and worked with me on the Water Board for a number of years. We had known each other since childhood and played together at school and at home, so when he passed away I was most upset and felt very sad when he was buried at Perranzabuloe churchyard.

'The following night, or early morning, I dreamt I was standing at Bob's grave, which is near the church tower (Bob was a bellringer), I was looking towards the east, across the fields behind the church where they slope down to the valley below. Dawn was breaking and I could just see the outline of the fields against the skyline. As I continued to face in that direction there appeared to rise from behind the top field where it met the sky, a huge silver ball just like a full moon coming up on the horizon, only a lot bigger and brighter. When it reached a certain height it exploded into thousands of particles which shot all over the still dark sky, just like a huge firework. Then I heard a voice speak from above, "Sorrow not for the body which lies below for Bob's spirit is here with me above." It was then I felt a great feeling of peace descend which seemed to disperse all sorrow.

'What I heard was, of course, quite true because the spirit, or soul, leaves the body at the time of death on this earth and goes on to another life of which we know nothing. The soul is immortal and takes with it the sum total of which we have done, or not done, throughout our life on this planet. I feel sure that if there is a life beyond this one, we will be judged according to our actions towards our fellow beings.

JACK Benney, dreamer of dreams. ▶

Fourth Dream

'This, the fourth and last dream, was very clear and vivid. I found myself walking along a road I have never seen in my waking life. Tall trees grew on either side blanking out the light of day. There was the smell of damp and rotting vegetation in the air (the sort of smell you get in woods in the late autumn or winter). On the right-hand side as I walked on was a very high stone wall, perhaps seven or eight feet in height, covered here and there with ivy and trailing brambles. The wall and the road suddenly took a right-hand turn, and I found myself walking up a slight incline, the trees on my left continuing with the road.

'Abruptly the wall ended with two high iron gates hung from granite posts. As I faced these gates I could see that the right-hand one was partly opened inwards and had come away from the top, hanging so that the gate had dropped with its end resting on the moss strewn path inside. The other gate remained in the shut position.

'After squeezing myself between the gates I found I was in a deserted churchyard; everywhere was overgrown with brambles, stinging nettles and ivy. The headstones were lichen covered and leaning in every direction. The church itself lay lower down to my right where a path led to a porch. It was in a ruinous state, the roof long gone. The tower was crumbling away, and ivy covered the whole length of the south side of the church from the ground to the top of the walls and up the tower: a scene of long disuse and decay.

'I now come to the reason why I came to this place of desolation: it was to go to a certain part of the churchyard. I seemed to know exactly where that was.

'When entering through the high iron entrance gates I had continued to walk straight ahead, not down towards the church. The path I was on ran parallel with the stone wall which also ran inwards at right angles to the road. I found I was making my way

◀ SKY and land meet at dusk on the beautiful Blackdown Hills.

down to the west end corner of the churchyard and approaching three headstones. These were identical, of square cut simple design, fashioned from grey slate. I knelt down in front of the middle one to read the wording cut deep into the slate memorial. I cannot recall all that was written there but this I do remember.

"Sacred to the memory of
John Curtis of this Parish who
passed away on July 15th, 1753
aged 67 years"

'By this time someone must have been standing behind me, although I did not turn around to see who it was, whether a man or a woman. This is what I said to the person standing there in that ancient and neglected burial spot – "That was once me who lies there, named John Curtis." I then awoke with total recall of that remarkable dream.'

MOST of us are curious about the future. Tarot card prediction is an area which has puzzled me. Isn't the fall of cards all luck and chance? I long held that view, but in 1974 I had an amazingly accurate reading by Pip Everard at Bossiney and, more recently, a reading by Shirley Wallis in our cottage near St Teath in 1986. By the end of the year most of the predictions made for Sonia and me had come true. Shirley, who lives at Plymstock on the edge of Plymouth, is the author of a fascinating book Discover the Tarot. *Her cards are photographed here. The origin of the Tarot lies in the mists of time, its true source a mystery.*

PSYCHIC POSTSCRIPT

A S I COME to the end of this journey, I count myself a lucky man.

Thanks to investigations, interviews and research into psychic phenomena over the last quarter of a century, I have met some fascinating people, found myself in some very unusual situations and, in seven words, have enriched the quality of my life.

Psychic matters have become an important part of my life, but by no means an obsession. The wise John Arlott once reflected 'What does he know of cricket who only cricket knows?'

I greatly appreciated Peter Underwood's inscription in his latest book *Ghosts & How to See Them:* 'For Michael Williams, searcher, researcher and balanced mind ... every good wish from the author.'

The contrasts of Bossiney publishing – cooking to murder, folklore to old photographs and a good deal more – in an area from Bristol across to Bournemouth and down to Land's End have all combined to give variety and a sense of perspective. And in off-duty hours there has been important work for animal welfare and pleasure in the encouragement of young cricketers for the Cornish Crusaders.

I hope to go on investigating the supernatural for the rest of my earthly life, and hope to be about when scientific evidence proves psychic phenomena really do occur in this world.

That will be a great moment.

MORE BOSSINEY BOOKS...

SUPERSTITION AND FOLKLORE
by Michael Williams. 44 photographs.
A survey of Westcountry Superstitions: Interviews on the subject and some Cornish and Devon folklore.
'...the strictures that we all ignore at our peril. To help us to keep out of trouble, Mr Williams has prepared a comprehensive list.'
Frank Kempe, North Devon Journal-Herald

STRANGE STORIES FROM DEVON
by Rosemary Anne Lauder & Michael Williams. 45 photographs.
Strange shapes and places, strange characters, the man they couldn't hang, and a Salcombe mystery, the Lynmouth disaster and a mysterious house are some of the strange stories from Devon.
'...full of good stories, accompanied by many photographs of local happenings which have mystified.'
Mary Richards, Tavistock Times

SUPERNATURAL INVESTIGATION
by Michael Williams
'...has to be the one you read in front of a roaring fire, curtains closed against the howling gale and a stiff whisky within arm's reach to calm the nerves.'
Wendy Hanwell, Tavistock Times

SUPERNATURAL IN SOMERSET
by Rosemary Clinch
Atmospheres, healing, dowsing, fork-bending and strange encounters are only some of the subjects featured inside these pages. A book, destined to entertain and enlighten – one which will trigger discussion – certain to be applauded and attacked.
'...an illustrated study of strange encounters and extraordinary powers...'
Somerset County Gazette

MYSTERIES OF THE SOUTH WEST
By Tamsin Thomas of BBC Radio Cornwall
A tour of ancient sites in Cornwall and on Dartmoor.
'There is little doubt that Tamsin Thomas has become the 'Voice of Cornwall.'
North Cornwall Advertiser

DORSET MYSTERIES
Bossiney invites six authors to probe mysterious facets of Dorset. The distinguished novelist Jean Stubbs, who sets the scene for *Dorset Mysteries* reflects 'This is a strange county, full of strange tales and superstitions.'

LEGENDS OF DORSET
by Polly Lloyd
The author explores legendary Dorset, visiting places as diverse as the Sacred Circle at Knowlton and Chesil Beach. Dorset is a mine of myth and folklore.
'Weird happenings...Polly Lloyd delves through tales ranging from moving rocks to murders.
Ed Perkins, Southern Evening Echo

GHOSTS OF DORSET
by Peter Underwood
The President of the Ghost Club explored a whole range of Dorset hauntings. A ghostly white donkey, a world-famous screaming skull, phantom coach-and-horses story which Thomas Hardy used in *Tess of the D'Urbervilles* and a prehistoric 'Peeping Tom' are some of the subjects.
Ghost hunter Peter Underwood has been spook stalking in Dorset uncovering a host of eerie brushes with the supernatural.'
Bournemouth Advertiser

STRANGE TALES OF THE SOUTH WEST
Ronnie Hoyle

GHOSTS AND PHANTOMS OF THE WEST
Peter Underwood

SOMERSET MYSTERIES
Polly Lloyd & Michael Williams

KING ARTHUR IN THE WEST
Felicity Young & Michael Williams

ABOUT EXMOOR
Polly Lloyd

CURIOSITIES OF EXMOOR
Felicity Young

We shall be pleased to send you our catalogue giving full details of our growing list of titles and forthcoming publications. If you have difficulty in obtaining our titles, write direct to Bossiney Books, Land's End, St Teath, Bodmin, Cornwall.